# *Pharmacopœia*
### &
### *Early Selected Works*

*Also by Elisabeth Bletsoe*

The Regardians: a book of angels
Portraits of the Artist's Sister
Pharmacopœia
Landscape from a Dream

# ELISABETH BLETSOE

# Pharmacopœia

&

*Early Selected Works*

Shearsman Books
Exeter

Published in the United Kingdom in 2010
by
Shearsman Books Ltd
58 Velwell Road
Exeter EX4 4LD

www.shearsman.com

ISBN 978-1-84861-082-8
First Edition

**Acknowledgements**

Many of these poems, or earlier versions of them,
appeared in the following:

*Cabaret 246, Calliope, Coal City Review* (USA), *Iota, Memes, Odyssey,
Orbis, Pennine Platform, Ramraid Extraordinaire, Scratch, Spectrum, Tears in
the Fence, Tenth Muse, Terrible Work, The Old Police Station, The Wide Skirt,
Writing for our Lives* (USA); website "The Tower of Silence"
(www.dhfurniss.eurobell.co.uk)

"Stinking Iris" appeared in *Neue Rundschau* (2008), translated into
German by Ude Strätling.

See also page 113.

# Contents

## Portraits of the Artist's Sister

## Individual Poems

## The Regardians

## PHARMACOPŒIA

## ACKNOWLEDGEMENTS     113

*For Ian*
*with my love*

# PORTRAITS OF THE ARTIST'S SISTER

*Based on the paintings, lithographs,
letters and diaries of Edvard Munch.*

## ALPHA AND OMEGA
*"seriously and jokingly tells the eternally recurring story"*

when you pulled me
from the mud,
Omega,
and woke me
touched me
with a fern frond
a green interrogation mark:
I could smell disaster,
the gunpowder between us

I must admit
I was really rather taken
with your eyes
which on ordinary days
were hyacinth
but when the serpent of desire
unwound your spine,
stormed black
in which red planets swam

we drank different coloured milk-shakes
walked by the sea for hours
brightness fell from the air
and the golden pillar of the moon
simmered on the water

I was happy, too happy
to write poetry
and so were you
(but that didn't matter
quite so much)

we made love in the woods
fell among the galaxies of
ramson flowers, dog's mercury;
our flesh bruised garlic

but then I caught you
talking with a SNAKE
you said that he was interesting
that there was nothing in it
no matter—
I squashed his head under my foot
while you were busy
among your many orchards

I know you said
you had to be creative
but for God's sake, Omega
you did it with a DONKEY
I thought you only meant
knitting
or macramé, something harmless
and just who was that BEAR
I came across—
he'd been fighting
with a heart-sick TIGER
for want of your body;
flesh hung in strips from the trees
and the ground was red
. . . and as for that PIG
I never would have thought
you'd have fallen for
someone with a curly tail
and such disgusting manners

in February you met
a poet-HYENA
with a shabby coat;
too concerned with the image
of being a poet
than with your true vision
your words of love left him
unmoved—
life could not touch him—
you made him a garland of flowers
while he drooped his head
disconsolate

it would have been easier
to take
if you hadn't had children
all those little monsters running round
with human heads
and furry limbs—
I wouldn't mind so much
if they didn't call me "father"

there wasn't a medical profession then
to create the concept of PMT
so I couldn't even blame it
on your hormones
when you wouldn't see the sense
of being ruled by me—
but when you eloped with that DEER
it was the last straw, so to speak
that broke the camel's back

Nature screamed.
The sunset bled across the sea,
ran howling up the beach.

I wrote bitter things about you
in bad verse
and left them scratched on leaves
and under stones
for worms and birds to read

I found you sleeping by the lake
I took you
and kissed you
under the glass coffin-lid of the water
until your lips sang bubbles
your face that was death-in-life
appalled me;
it wore the same look
as when I met you first

and now your beauty ringing out
a great drowned bell
telling my deed
and, Omega, the animals
your children and your friends—
their eyes burn red holes in the shadows
the ground shakes with their tread.
I love you now, Omega,
now you are safe and dead
but it was when you said
it was when you said
you loved me—
then I feared you most

## THE VOICE
*dream of a Summer night*

Never when eyes are looking at you
can you find them beautiful,
remark their colour;
they are hidden by the other's look.

Silent regardian,
your gaze is Possession, since at once
you cause my being and steal it from me;
fashioning my body in its nakedness,
sculpting that which I shall never see,
holding the secret of what I am.

My longing had no shape; flexuous,
warping, it was the shoreline's milk-dust path,
at times a wooden boat, white-hulled,
a lake of azuline.

What is desire but this revelation of your eyes,
the fact of my own flesh? My touch,
in turn, invites you to yourself; reciprocal,
we are doubly incarnate.

Nothing between us
but the burning wires of the afternoon;
rapture, to hear oneself say "now", to brush together
our lips' dry tinder, ignite the moment
with our single spark and torch to ashes round us
the melting, breathless trees.

## THE SOLITARY ONE

not lonely, but alone
in the grisaille of evening
the light-haired woman of spring
dreaming towards life

day and night commingled:
       a moment of balance
       and impending change
             sways the magic mirror

                  suspended

by a ripple
her image lies beyond where
fabulous stones birth at the surface
             with their white laughter

way, way out there
the soft line where ocean
                blends with air
incomprehensible as existence
eternally longing:

a grey attenuation of cloud

           darkling,
the sea becomes more vast
               with possibility:
       amethystine of her pleasure

oh  and up there, the moon
barely perceptible

later to emerge
    a discreet pollen
        on a blue hour

# PORTRAITS OF THE ARTIST'S SISTER

*I. sister inger*

Caught on the thorn between moment and moment,
this woman is on the point of entry
or departure.

Resonant with music of objects unseen,
what blessings or doomed oracles
beat up against such nun-close lips?

Though her face is a door
swung open onto night,
her eyes,
receiving visions of earth's calvaries,
brimful, betray a doubtful, drowning spring.

Outside an ancient snowbird
claps its freezing wings.

Austerity threatens
to overwhelm the star-flake brooch,
those anxious hands.

*II. inger on the shore*

white folds of your dress
uninterrupted by love;
hat barring your lap

your back to the waves,
you borrow strength from the rock,
chainless and alone

half-moon aspect; where
other women are many
you, of all, are one

*III  portrait of inger*
*mood in colours of black and violet*

a wound in air
through which light implodes

blank as a vampire's mirror
she permits no shadows

hands a tight dahlia
ten twisted petals

straight, smooth-skulled
like a match she waits

for one to strike her
make her head a blaze

## PUBERTY

started while riding
a horse called Rufus

red banner
on white linen

no celebration

might as well have
pricked my finger
                on a spindle
& gone to sleep for a 100 years

burying rusted pants
                in the back garden
binding my breasts
with torn strips
                to force them back

refusing food
as part of an effort to
                *stay the same*

used to watch
the mirror for hours
moon-face swam up
                to greet me
changing daily
                (mainly ugly)
saying "do you know who
you really are?"

unable to stand
the presence of father
his all-seeing Eye

hating mother because
    she knew
        and didn't tell

cried because I didn't
    want to be twenty
        and my life over

felt the stares of
all the local boys
    each time I lay down

fragments of lycanthropy
    in the dark
when I discovered my own pleasure
and *what you could do with it*

ashamed
    (even now):

        of this
        my shadow-side

## MADONNA

lotus of the palace of water,
daughter of the reconcilers;
her silence the groaning of ice

opaque glass receiving all images,
retaining none; like death
she is a mirror that flatters not

cold, fish-chaste; behold
how she approaches,
a lovely dwindling shape
scooped from winter flesh

the hellish Holy; beware
her rosy garland,
the crown of thorns, bloodbeads
that spring from her yielding

# THE LADY WITH THE BROOCH

*I Madonna*
*(fantasy)*

                    separately
he examines each eyelash —
those green nuances in the iris
that have the sea's transparency —
her pupils large in the half-light —
          twin dark heavens
towards which his soul spirals
                    like smoke from sacrificial fires

touching her mouth with his finger—
          the soft flesh yields
          as her lips move into a smile—
                    reflecting red lights
her brooch a circling of panther's eyes

he imagines her face
          raked by moonlight;
blood-filled, her pomegranate lips
a woman who gave herself away
                    to obtain a grievous beauty

          earth's Madonna
bringing forth her children in pain—
in her mouth's corner a spectre of death
                    in her two lips the joy of life

## II *The violin concerto*
*(reality)*

you are a river of music, he says
in which he yearns to lave
his soul's sickness

the photograph over his bed
a powerful transducer of
        his emotional energy
talisman against his own limping devils

hands braid invisible threads
his heart dangles on wires of fantasy
        but "his" Eva
                is enthralled by Bella—
an "unnatural" passion he cannot comprehend—
a love that strikes like lightning
        forbidden
                and reversed

meeting in Berlin
she is distant, artificially polite
choosing words with decorum
        like an offended queen—
against his will almost
he can only draw her as Salome
dealer in death, in which his mandrake art
                takes root—
     "Man's Head
            in Woman's Hair"

she struggles over his handwriting—
is this what he meant when he said
           the sexes have
                     no mutual understanding?

at the Hotel Sans Souci
he fills her room with equipment—
a double portrait
that never seems to materialise—
the two women angered, oppressed
by the mute presence of
           a lithographer's block—
the brief note attached:
                "THIS is the stone
                          that fell
                               from my heart"

## THE BEAST

when you arrive
I put my hand up to my face
as if you were distant
a forest fire

useless it is
to quench your image
with green thoughts of shadows
rippling over skin,
curl of wild cress
and long spears of night rain

peculiarly scarlet
your blood must be:
lashing your ribs
leaping like dark butterflies to your lips
lacing your torso with a running flame

under the heavy fell of hair
your face being set
with a red look:

jaguarundi

your cat heat smell
peppers
my raw wet membranes:
taking the measure
of your pug-marks
but you are always turned
in another direction
skirt hitched

replenishing the fields
with your deciduous womb:

She-Ranter, provoker of hierarchies

knowing this to be true
that the heat of your lust
is not for the timid
I cast myself down
in the dust
in the door of the leper's hospital
to lick
your naked foot

## VAMPIRE

I come from a darker mountain
than yours,
a colder fjord:
let me slip with my skin
pull you in with my arms, my white arms
that are whiter than sleeping in snow

no he said no; you
are a broken instrument

take my hair, my red hair
make it a bright bonfire
let the flames creep over you dancing
eating up your little love, your offerings
you bring to the altar of my body

and he said too wild your music is

take my breasts that are perfumed
all over with rain; they are
two secret terrible birds
to tear you joyfully

and he said yes

take my lips that are shaped
to suck the breath from your mouth;
inside I shall be deep roses of fire,
in each heart a star of blood

and he said yes he said yes
yes I will

## MOONLIGHT

*"on evenings like this I could do anything—something terribly*
*wrong"*

the dumb supper is prepared;
a meal cooked without salt
while the sun rolls minutely round
under neap tides

blind crayfish thoughts crawl
from her neglected waters as
dark Hel-energies drive her
from the House; its foundations
shored up with neuroses and
denial of heart rest

she is now beyond the pale
where blackness is thick, like fur
and the great grey-faced owl
murders, a moon on wings—
this joy drinks deeper than delight

offering herself to an inner, lunar light
suffering its transformations;
a speculum in which to view herself
confronting her woman's shape:
an unknown woman
an endless shadow woman
a fateful encounter woman
woman of night-haunted beauty

waiting
for the wave of darkness, crimson-lined,
to curl and crest about her
to breach the manufactured whalebone walls

release her from the stiff, silk castle

                                        of her dress
to float her breasts and hair upon eternity
and kiss a wide red smile upon her bloodless lips:
the wounded healer at the crossroads
opening the portals to a second life

loosely shrouded in delicious white
not a ghost, but a Sister
she sails her broken eggshells
over an ocean of night

## WOMAN IN BLUE

on the clearest days
certain women hold their peace,
angelic, trembling

in danger's face
they smile an inner smile
withholding small sins

their goal is attained,
the horizon no longer
though it remains blue

# THE DEAD MOTHER

and death comes
as this bluish distillate
in the base of an old
                    cracked cup

the heart adrift

frost-fern on glass; last
breath now
                    crystalline

the mild tyranny of
kissing the dead
as they would have wished it
more in life

"having lifted
          the veil
I will cover my face
                    again"

grief as *process*

                         alarm

speaking in
whispers "in case
          reality
becomes too real"

                    searching

"for weeks & weeks
I couldn't bear
       the light"

           mitigation

anger & guilt; learning
the cost of commitment


imaging the dead in
a series of pictures, each
bleeding into/replacing
       another
a thousand kaleidoscope
           fragments
until with one twist
we view them
       finally whole
*"flying?*
*as they sometimes were—?"*

irresistible changes
that Spring
       reminds you of:
cautiously we watch
the hands,
       the skin


dry twigs struggling
towards the inevitable;
their soft invasions
having long made indistinct
       the paths
           between the trees

## PORTRAIT OF ANNE BUHRE
*For C. T.*

weaving
the fabric of the poem
around her mystery;

concealing a cipher, her form
a coalescence once latent
beneath the painted surface

impasto
of September's greens & auburns, adrift
on an updraught,

richness of horse chestnut, lightly gummed;
luminosity of Sulphur Tuft &
nectarine-scented gills of Russula

luteal days, on the cusp
of autumn's menses;
the impenetrable dissimulations of the heart

in guise of iridescent raven
with woodland hair
upswept,

the storm-woman enters,
a charming rainmaker, proclaiming
let the equinoctials begin!

# ROSE AND AMÉLIE

tongues pickled in their own vinegar
they squat
rustling their big breasts
over the dried figs of their genitals

sisters

with cruel carmine smiles
they cheat each other at whist
invent each other's fortunes

the slap, slap of cards
absorbed into the eternal sepia
of four o'clock in the afternoon

the creaking joists of conversation settle

there goes the three of hearts
the queen of swords
*la maison Dieu*
death

the heads nod, shoulders roll together

agree:
it's good to dredge
the darker side of life
occasionally

## GIRLS ON A BRIDGE

this gossip is good
        to hear;
all this talk of oak
           and stone
wish-wives, like honey-spilling
hives we are, men stand amazed
        at our buzzing heads

we pick out the one voice
from the river's
        many voices
we never lose our thread

weaving fabrics for our
skirts that the winds
        rustle;
sewing tissue to bone
        and bone to muscle

we know how to cook
        and dazzle,
mix milk and menses,
        acorns, eggs:
boil them up in our kettle

we write in secret
we can bleed
        and not die

we know how to
shake the snow from a blanket
        make the feathers fly;

when the time is ripe, we'll
take the bread from the oven

we know where the heart lies,
where the roots of a great tree
                feed on decay;
where the city grows back
                beyond its branches

and we know this also:

that the thread that is broken
                means death

## AMOR AND PSYCHE

*"male-and-female created he them"*

enlightenment began
with an act of disobedience:

betrayed and betraying
I could not contain
the oil-leap within;
the flame of consciousness
seared you that lay on the wick,
the hooded stranger

you fled
I sought but found you not;
drawing a blank,
a veil over my head

among bones, among shards
I dug in the dirt
explored the interior,
the midden, the memoried matrix;
myself re-membered
in the myth-mouthing mothering dark

*my substance not hid from thee*
*when I was made and curiously wrought*
*in the lowest parts of the earth*
ripening; a seed under my tongue,
learning love's language

overwhelmed in a welter
overturned on an ocean;
a wave, a wilful wife,
weaving my way towards you

with bliss-heavy gait,
passing, eager-footed,
to the circle desired

returned and returning
reconciled in reflection;
the wax and wane
of a twin-headed axe

soul-image, I am;
new moon in your heart

fearfully and wonderfully made

# Individual Poems

## WATCHET

blue lias
rock
the cliffs
"Watchet-blue"

*Celtic Venture*
brings timber
    from Lisbon
takes lumber back
    Thursday

nostalgia of
wallflowers
that
estuarine smell

the endless
amiabilities of
ripple-theory
    flickering
interfluence of sea
& rivercurrent

entero-
morphia:
new weeds
make delicate
shapes; stars,
fern-boats,
lettuce,
string

a
woman alone
    collecting
among pebbles &
housebricks worn
    ovoid

"Robert"
starting to build
    a dam
arresting the flow
but not
    stopping it

these "fontal truths"
& a pair
of mallards
    breasting
the waves
  very
    jollily

## AN OBLIQUE LOOK THROUGH WATER
*for Ruth*

held
in a reticle of light
water
& a wood-pigeon's

   scalloped flight

how precisely to catch—
that is to say
a certain "brilliance"

occurrence
& reoccurrence of

small
volcanic eruptions of

& ropes of sand
twisting
   untwisting

that skein
   always
across my perception

opacities like
elver-swarms feeling that
vertiginous
   lunar tug

with parallels
"moving strongly towards"
cross-hatched
by wind-diagonals

        & then

to reconstruct
the sound of a tossed pebble
from the surface resonance
        ringing out

        bringing to bear upon

the oscillations
of the little yellow buoy

        *Penarth Pier*

## Low Season, Whitby

*I Saltwick Nab*

at shore-level
entering with microscope
I produce this for you:
a clot of mica,
quartz and calcite,
whelk chips,
arteries, alveoli of green/mauve weeds;
a mussel, hair-glued
to a half-inch core of blackwrack

your corners already filled
with such dehydrated memories;
indulgent, you focus your telescopic lens
on the red legs of oystercatchers

brown-strapped *Lamonaria*,
fruiting bodies of *Fucus*, volatile
with oils, mineral traces
and mucilage

my mouth tasting salt &
Helena Rubenstein's *Rose Indienne*;
your tongue a cold muscle,
the saline foot of a shellfish:

outline of a sunken boat
in the grey ribbing of water

*II Providence*

too mild for January
breakdown of the ozone layer
no doubt,
heralding a spring of monstrous births,
two-headed calves &
unfavourable omens in the sky

as a single magpie tips its tail
over the hedge,
the teeth of a great black dog
snap at my heel
through High Hawsker;

vertebrae of the Abbey
constantly before us
as we walk a corkscrew path
on the wrong side of the looking glass

fish-scale skies &
the unbelievable violence of the sunset
changed the colours in your eyes
and stuck in my throat

when suddenly
the air was full of angels
being a blueish colour
about the bigness of a capon
having faces (as we thought)
like owls

*III The Pier-head Abandoned*

every movement now
has significance beyond its meaning;
dancing
in peacock-blue lycra tights
by the empty bandstand,
the locked fortune-teller's booth
to a tune more counterpoint
than strictly harmony

*IV Talisman*

all windows plead "Vacancies";
on formal lawns
staccato of *Galanthus nivalis*,
"the snow-piercer"

rolling out of the Board Inn,
three ammonites set in the wall
by Abbey steps; a talisman
against witches, wind & weather,
against being bit
        by Three Biters:
eye,
        tongue
                & heart
ocular fascination
bitter words
malevolence concealed

## THE ALEMBIC

full circle
the year's wheel

hedgerows
buoyant ashstems &
quick silver-
dark hollythorn

equivocal, the
fields of plover;
    solstice-birds
concealing
        new secrets
the piebald
    of magic &
        deception:
soot versus frost

on the wet sand
the sun's pillar
    shattered
& Gabriel's footsteps
    bloodstained
        & golden

draining the sky
    pebbles
absorbing colour
give back
    dull mauve,
duck egg blue

in the small wind
an interstitial
    scratching
        & knocking,
spume torn
from the wave's edge

attempts at reading
signs & symbols in
the dinosaur tracks
    of gulls,
Devonian tide-marks

alchemical days:
a process of
self-transformation
    with
your love the touchstone
changing
    everything

*Rhossili Bay, 24/12/92*

## ST BRIDGET'S

*"dog-faced, she moans in the churchyard"*
*for Andrew Jordan*

            slowly
she reveals herself
        from
the pyramid of firs:
beacon of black light
on the flat of the land

nettles infest her;
glass warping
in thick waves through which
        the centuries
                are bent

out
of kilter
        & sinking
in the alluvium

barbed wire
forbidding trespass
that "noe man
        with me mell"
*vagina dentata,* all
turned in on herself
                today

bees in orbit;
electrons about a nucleus
& she the queen of
        these transformed
                witches:

an oracular swarm

the ground is humming
      & dangerous, radials
running through the grass
            pigeons
erupt from the belfry
& from nowhere
    a boy
vaults quickly back over
with face
        a maze

tower
      cracked wide
by a bolt from
          Mary Lucifer
stone saints
      break into leaf:
a destruction of forms
an unfettering
opening the way
      that
leads to the centre

         placing
my hand  on the porch wall
in recognition
       of a sense of flow
my occult blood &
the new moon sat
         in the arms of the old

*St. Brides, Wentlooge,*
*Gwent*

# DEER SEEN FROM A TRAIN NEAR DILTON MARSH

snowspittle
evanescent
     in sunlight

chalk sustains
the first
chilly primulas

chiaroscuro
of ash-saplings
     half-concealing
legs more slender,

bone-mettled
at engine's onslaught
the sprung energy
of a leap
     arrested

transposed
along the tensile nerves
towards barely perceptible
     uplift of head

the dark muzzle;
eyes almond-slanted &
     startled as
my own reflection
     trapped
     within the glass

# Notebooks Retrieved From The Sea

(1)    Gifts from the sea
and what can we exchange
in return for lemons,
a bottle of Spanish brandy
and ghosts of crabs
the size of my fingernail?

Water dark green,
crawling white:
we watch its slow
and magical transformation
into that rain-cloud
on Llanmadoc Hill.

(2)    The dunes harbour
invisible stings.

Lilac-veined, the sea-holly
a frilled lizard,
vaunting.

Its spines pierce the sky which
bleeds a little.

Pollen and sand.

(3)    200 feet above sea-level,
guardians of the stone cists,
the neolithic dead,

inhabit our bodies
bickering:
old feuds discharging
at the surface of history
while from here
undercurrents are revealed
in shades of jade and beryl.

Your footprints infill
as they are made.


(4)    Dreamt I woke to find a woman
reading aloud from
a book with no words,
holding her right hand in greeting
to the sun and the sea.

The sea turned into a carnival,
became a multitude
and a horned man
with caprine eyes
embraced me, saying:
"you are now, and have always been
one of us".


(5)    The castle of winds
a poor defence:
swallows and martins
infest the solar, salt
nibbles the limestone.

The small fire on the beach
cannot prevail against
encroachments of spindrift and haar.

Twilight.
A ring of blackened stones.


(6)      Angel of the sea
wrecked
by a fall of Perseids;

black and white feathers
float, suspended.

Nets of mackerel light.


(7)      Spokes of colour
wheel through the water (like)
the language of cuttlefish.

Cloud-shadows.

Reflected, the sun becomes
a moon: menstrual and
swollen with radiance.

Violet hills hung
on the tail of a Chinese kite.


(8)      Not so much a drowning
as a loss of identity; both
effortless.

Pelvic girdle of coast
constricting,
the lochial waters.

Not to touch bottom
in the lee of a wave, or
perceive my body
under the surface:
a swimming head,
Orphic.

Foam-gagged and blinded:
the fear without you
on the empty sea.


(9)     Beached waves,
        stranded jellyfish.

        Pushing my fingers in
        to these blue medusas;
        the mouth, the labial maze.

        Soft polyps.

        How to comprehend this,
        so immaculate and imprecise,
        curd of condensed sea-water?

(10)    As many tinctures up here as
        heathers in the sea;

        August evening on the downs.

Between gaps, an iridescence;
shall we call it "shot silk"?

Our ragged descent
into darkness;
nightshade, those white plume moths.

*"What else does one hope for;*
*after all?"*


*Llangennith Burrows, Rhossili*

# THE REGARDIANS

*Angels cluster and rustle just to the side of my vision.*
Lee Harwood

*Then said I, O my lord, what are these? And the angel that talked with me said unto me, I will shew thee what these be. And the man that stood among the myrtle trees answered and said, These are they whom the Lord has sent to walk to and fro through the earth.*
Zechariah 1:9:10

*". . . angels who clatter their gills to sign and speak the names of future edens"*
Brian Catling

**regardian** (rê gar' di ân) [F. *regarder* (RE-GUARD); O.F. *gardien*, from *garde*, n. Portmanteau word indicative of two functions e.g. of an angel or spirit; one who looks at, observes, notices, gives heed to or takes into account; one who charge, care, or custody of any person or thing, acting as a guardian or protector.

## ARCHANGELIS
*Michaelmas poem, September 29th, 1991*
*For Louise*


in separating, you diminish


archangelis
      down from your hill
             into Glamorgan vale
the church named for you
        Llanvihangel:
this tower's fossil coil of stairs
and ritual chants from vandal crows
      signify
                 your conquest of the pagan
thrusting
your divisive blade
      into the dragon's mouth,
          the dark vulva of earth;
you have turned her moon-face
      to its dark side:
no more healing at the well
now Kore sits      grieving
awaiting the flowering of the depths
no more hart's tongue or bird's nest
ground elder and guelder rose:
you have made her Black Annis,
      storm-hag,
          devourer of children

only the diseased lung of a fallen maple
putting out dried leaves of blood
    and the phrase from the open Bible
        that worked in me like a thorn:
*you eaters of flesh by twilight*


look how Crivelli saw you:
lions roaring from your cuissed thighs
bouncing        bare toed
on the scaly chest of the spiderous demon,
    his red tongue squirting
and a diminutive Adam and Eve
weighed in your balance
        and found wanting


you read in the book of my soul
crossing the t's
and correcting the grammar
Michael
you've been measuring since the Fall
who said God
        was in the details?


        Satan
hurled flaming headlong down
    into the river Taff;
his mirror-image flown
        under the surface
thus rendering all things reflective
        dangerous

pure in your cruelty
sheathing your sword in Rome
I can feel you coming, with all
        your Miltonic armies
as moderate westerlies increase
the patio door    slams shut
cold front nosing towards Scandinavia
      the hem of your feathered cloak
           crisping the trees auburn
setting ragwort flares among the horse dung
untended bonfires
         filling the air with ash
*the harvest is over*
    *the summer is ended*
        *and we are not saved*


who now observes your fast these
burnt out ember days?
odour of lamb's blood
broken bread    no more
bull-baiting
    shin-kicking
        cudgel-fighting lammas fairs
in your honour:
    the dancing
is finished, the mummers
      went home long ago
only coincidental fireworks over Cardiff Bay
      even they were rained off


september
is boys in maroon blazers
      treading wet pavements

craneflies struggling against panes of light
a woman brushing
     fallen lime leaves
          from a pram


Saturn in my solar house
a time for discipline
     to develop boundaries
pondering the words of an oriental princess:
"there has been no change
but I am no longer young
     autumn wind blows and
          I am as disturbed as before"


lord of the elements of fire
I am lighting a candle
to afford your protection
     what price now
          an escort to paradise?

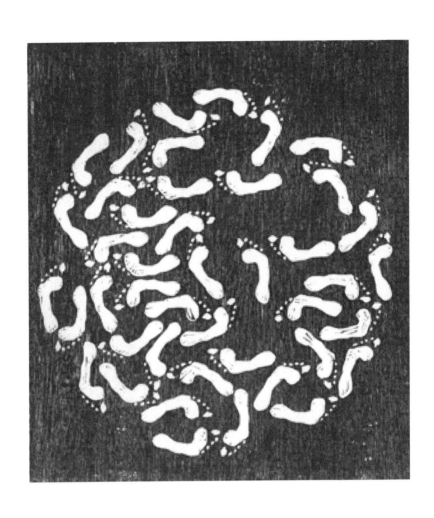

## THE 'OARY MAN

follow my gab'el, 'oary man
"the glorious mover in the circle"
a whirling priest possessed; a congregation
                    caught in your orbit
            setting in motion
                    a perpetual river of dance


your restlessness
a rhythmic ebb and flow of energy
bringing a process to action:
                    lunar horn
            waxing toward the solstice,
part spirit, part spiritually
                    inchoate,
            bound to fulfilment


writer of footsteps
                    on the day's edge
I find your traces
        over the park gates
in a frosted scrollwork of ivy,
translucent globes
                    dependent
from a tangle of bare thorns:


a reversal of tides
shifts currents of thought and feeling
        love-ties
suffering a sea-change
as out of the chestnut woods

a myriad sounds of water
like thousands of tiny chandeliers
        dropping:
a burst of milder weather
        coming in from the south-west


in apparent waste land
the spade rings on hard earth,
        a page stays unwritten in my head,
the slow course of seeding fresh perceptions
                        draws us to sleep;
secret works being wrought underground
in rhizomes,
        corms & bulbils
the poem                the swollen belly
        ideas
thrust into consciousness
        by the radical English dreamers
                who claimed your authority:
the Fiery Roll inscribed with blueprints
        for a world
                        turned upside-down


                        *non timere*
your messages pulse
                over the radio-waves
to old tramps wedged in shop doorways
        & those who wait
                in the dole-queues;
your skeins of geese still yelping across the sky
        (though their numbers may be counted):
the heart's wild huntsman

in constant pursuit       the sacrificial beast
          brought to its knees
                    in the lap of a virgin,
     a salvation
     a future self-greening
against the continual death of the body:


                    Christ's mass
light strobes through scattering pines
          hones itself on the earth's rim
                    at the low point of the year
Milky Way a faint lactation
as rival groups of carol-singers in Severn Road
                    set up a counterpoint
Plough hanging over the chimney
ladles great lungfuls of freezing air
                    straight from the Pole:


     nail-star
round which the great world-tent
          revolves


demon-gatherer,
          enemy of the Leviathan
on the last day you will still attend us,
                    a faithful spirit;
when the first three evening stars appear
          the prayer invokes you;
                    I wait
     on your circuitous arrival

and, like the door in the moon,
                my heart stands
        a little ajar for you


                    this soulless month

## THE LEAFY SPEAKER

Angel,
you break through the hedge
in your wide-brimmed hat
and call to me:
a startling epiphany
though your feet seem solid enough
on the unremarkable pavement

juggling
with all those wordy elements
an overhead cascade of
devil-sticks and pentacles
the life-force lightly tossed
with matter
descending
pattern, rhythm and stress
in perpetual states of becoming
could flip right out
anytime
this twirling chaos of delight
existing only as a form of play
the sheer weight of the senses
an illusion you create:
"the fluidic basis of all transmission
of activity"

hearing your names
in a shuffle of tarot
Thoth                    Tehuti
Merlin                              Mercurius
snake-tattooed
in full pentecostal dress
crescent moons jingling in your pocket

                        gold in your left ear
or, roosting naked
        in an ash tree
as darkness fades,
        a galaxy of freckles
                        on your sleeping back
sunlight
exploding yellow pollen-stars
on the pussy-willow

at Fforest-fawr,
beech trunks muscular pillars of
        a drowned cathedral
wave of the woods about to crest
        light & sappy
flowing on down Coed-y-Wenallt
to Rhiwbina's suburban gardens where
you close over
        raw wet rolls of mud
saffron-smear of smashed crocus:
heal the ragged places in me that
the wind tears through
        "zero at the bone:"
the sometime bitterness of spring

                again
that feeling of anticipation
as if a hand gently squeezed
        the spongy density of my lungs

you show me the world
        in reverse
teach me the alphabet of surprise
after a sudden downpour
                        ankle-deep in sky

trees rooted in themselves
      birds returned once more
            to fish in flight:
the red lion shall become white
      and the white eagle red
the pale prince and black princess
lock lips
      and merge
salt to silver
and sulphur to gold

love, even when lost
becomes condensed
directing my ways of being
      from inside
          and deep down

your departures leave on the air
a bruised space
      the city
echoes, re-echoes with your image
your stone face leans down from
          the Lutheran churchhouse
branches
      in rhyming couplets
stream from your mouth
          leafily speaking
the greene man the holy oake
all that is ancient and mute
you give tongue to:
      *a vision of the world*
          *before the world*

turning my body in sleep
entering me through dreams

pouring into my ears
         your wild and tender stories
your gaze a grey dawn
on volcanic shores
                beautiful stranger

I think as though I spoke
         to someone in my head
*inside closed eyes*
*close the eyes once more*
*then even the stones*
                *will come alive*

## THE CLOUDSEEDER

you are a violent messenger
though I'm not beyond your charms
"one of his most potent memories
                    was of me
leaning out the bathroom window
bare arms to the night
and just letting the storm"


nothing more delicious than
          the smell of rain
                    on hot pavements

a lifting of air over the squall fronts
forerunners arching
                    & scudding
intense potential energy of
          the cumulonimbus
                    its tower-clouds
lightning-veins breaking toward the zenith:
cameo shot of my neighbour
shovelling hailstones
                    alone in the dark


your hand beats on the taut sky
over one of the country's hottest cities:
in the pedestrian precinct
I turn to avoid the street-theatres
          outdoor cafés
                    winos & Italian students
tasting the beginnings of sickness
as blue gases drift from North Road

you move among us
                    intent
with polished limbs of brass
your hair a burning bush
          and your voice
                    the voice of the crowd


smog warnings on local radio
as the laser cuts St. Mary Street:
above dark vibratory horizons
          the white Portland stone of
"one of the loveliest city centres
                    in Europe"
still manages to rise
          casual as thistledown



immobile parklands where
baked stones carry their UV memories
                    into the evening
at the edge of the river where
it is no longer permitted to swim:
          hanging
blunt-nosed shadows of infrequent trout
     & small detonations from
                    the seed-pods of balsam



air at blood-heat and tacky
to the point where thought unravels,
          the thin red line:
Ely riots &
          purple clematis blooms
                    tap at the window

creation theories and
    the big bang the
    big crunch put
a million archangels out of work
now God is up for grabs and
the quickest way to heaven is
        a night-club & an oral dose
            of ecstasy


you slope off with your sandwich board
        over the bubbling tarmac
wherever your neon eyes rest
the writing appears on the wall
*and the fourth angel poured out his vial*
            *upon the sun*
*and power was given unto him*
*to scorch men with fire*
*and men were scorched*
            *with great heat*


and Bateson had said in the sixties
that in thirty years
the ice-caps would melt & inundate
            continents:
threats of invasion by unkind forces
sky falling out all around
        while trees stand like
            hosts of withered seraphim


moon slung over Atlantic Wharf
half-eaten, obscured by blood, with
wild tides ravaging the coasts
        flooding the reens & valleys

how we make our own condition
the action          politic
"that which is prudent or
          expedient"


I dreamed last night
          I fought with you
                    upon the mountainside
drops of your sweat fell
                    and ran
along my underlip; hip to hip
          a climax, a rain of blows
those tender bodyshocks
          before you flew away

               and were no more

## LACHRIMATORY
*"Sorrow is both season and place" (Rilke)*

opened the door
found my soul stuffed
    full of dead wings

the solace, at least
of lifting one's head
    out here in the open

Victorian spire
penetrates the cloud
and by cloud is itself
            dissolved:
a leaden humidity

overfilled river twisting and
            moth-like
the undersides of the white poplar
flash the sibilants of your name
        Cassiel


angel of broken marriages
    old photographs
all those dead letters sent
the failure of my days
        the years
the single abandoned glove
    at the roadside:
mislaid my own twenties
in some interior
        crying

your timeless downward gaze
merely logged on file the
sadnesses accumulating
    under my eyelids

your followers the living suicides
those ghosts of flesh
marked out by the knowledge they will
    in all probability
        die at their own hand


cathedral now a broken hull of light
an upturned boat of a saint
    Christ the Majestas
with his "distressingly Jewish nose"
    and erotic feet
roped to the mast among
the caulked spirits of the dead
sailing the dark side of his passage;
a drenched Satan claws at the keel
    choking on shadows
        thrown in his teeth
neck-veins like muscled ivy
    bulging
      and me wondering
could you get lit up about evil
    once in a while?

you  feign disinterest
manicure your disciplined hands that
I dare not take for fear of
    encroachment upon
        your chastity
chortling of the storm-drains

as water runs
        from the umbrella
                into my shoe
last chord of the Magnificat washing out
under the carved dripstone
leaving the air
                shocked


elder, sorb, yewberry
the season's sour essence:
wild raspberries leak blood
        in the cemetery
where crazy tilted headstones
record histories of aborted hopes
infant mortality, epidemics,
        the outbreak of war
instruments of Passion ranged on the tomb-top
the nails, the sponge, the scourge
                neat as pencils


you have the smile of a civil servant
leaning your elbows on a parapet
        in your bespoke overcoat;
pole tilts toward the equinox and
the world grows grey from your breath;
your final demands for restraint, redress
        the settlement of debts
                wait unopened on the mat


coffee and welshcakes in the prebendary
        hemmed in by rain
the Close becomes a dangerous reflection
                of itself
wrought-iron lamppost piping silver

                along the Dean's steps
an electric aureola around each leaf

            adolescent laughter
rapid-fire spores of lust in
                        the muscoid dark
shreds of porn magazines
            pulp in the hedge
the shucked skin of a rubber
under a memorial bench
            voyeurism
just part of the government job:
                        you know
Heaven and Hell are the same place
all the suppressed beatings
of your enshrouded heart
cannot disguise
            your secret joy
                        in falling

# AZRAEL

*"to bear all death, the whole of death, death even*
*before life, and gently, without rancour*
*to keep it contain it,*
*is terrible beyond all language"* (Rilke)


MYSTERY MAN KNOCKED SENSELESS IN S. WALES
not everyone loves a blue angel
I met you once
                    on a railway footbridge
a black Alsatian-cross with
pricked ears
        long lupine jaws
                    & eyes like peeled grapes, but
I was not ready
    I let you pass
you growled somewhere
            deep in your throat-fur

number me the unfavourable omens:
magpie rattles in St. Catherine's churchyard;
a black and white skin, rusty with old blood,
        slaps at the air from a washing-line;
broken alphabet of bird-dance against toppling clouds;
back-seat rape on a deserted highway;
conifer twigs
        caught in the clothes of a hanged bride;
unidentified corpse under Pontsarn viaduct;
adolescent with knives
        threatens his mother's lover;
chalk shadow drawn on the steps of a nightclub;
the stink of sulphur
        from long-neglected drains in King's Road;
a blossoming of posters from "The Third Position",
        thinly-disguised fascism;

anti-Jewish graffiti wounding the carnival walls;
the puddle of low-level radioactivity
            that is Roath Lake;
**CARDIFF RAID BID MAN IN DEATH PLUNGE**

*there's danger on the edge of town,*
                    *baby*

Witness
            Record
                        Assess
                                    Preserve

Garth mountain engulfed by your dark oesophagus
with joyous teeth clenched tight on your hunger
grinding the stars into chromosomes
though fewer people nowadays, if at all
                        seem beautiful

                        wintermoon
blue siren-scribble across pavements that are
            glittering snowfields of mica
half-fall of jazz-notes
            from an open window in Cathedral Road;
                        they burst lightly on impact
flickering arctic light in one corner of every room
holding a viewer to ransom:
**HEADLESS TORSO IN RIVER SHOCK**
            you hitch your wings
measuring out their lives with a titanium rod

in the lines on your palm
the topography of avarice and discontent

that is the city
**CARDIFF HIT BY FIREBOMB TERROR**
above its white noise you detect
a multiplicity of others' thoughts
        rippling through you
in variegated emotional colours;
communicatory pulses in the mantle
of a giant cephalopod, drifting
        in a vast sky-bed
feeling souls like fingerprints
        rolling them up into pellets
                        of their original clay


easy enough to tell the heart of a murderer


**VIRUS ORIGINS IN OUTER SPACE CLAIM**
under your aegis
feel the tug of the dirty snowball of frozen gas
in its long Plutonian orbit
revealing a need
                        to bring to the surface
that which incoheres,
                the root of neurosis
**BODY IN CARPET FOUND IN SHALLOW GRAVE**
society works at
        extruding its demons
as withered mammoths
        buttercups still in their mouths
are disgorged by the movements of glaciers:
plough it back,
        the rage and the lust


powerhouse,
your engines driven by deep rock strata
        magma fissures

the nine-tenths of the iceberg unconscious
sin-eater, gorging on evil
and spewing it up
        in the shape of a hard-won truth
if it were possible to confront your ugliness
you would relinquish a gift:
        regard for life
        space for grief
                the art of dying well


ice on the roof-tiles
a long grey flight feather blows
into the hallway
once again I see you have
        passed over
empty carapace of sky offering no clue
        to your whereabouts
no emergent solution to the riddle
WHO WATCHES THE WATCHMEN?

# GLOSSARY FOR *THE REGARDIANS*

**Archangelis**: St. Michael is the warrior-archangel who threw Satan from heaven and who was responsible, subsequently, for destroying sites of pagan worship. His once thriving cult, which overlaid that of Lug the Celtic god of Light, is now forgotten. The angel who judged the life of a person after death and escorted them either to heaven or to hell; often depicted trampling the devil; the prototype of St. George. Michael-churches (in Welsh, Llanfihangel) are often built on a hilltop, but in the poem the church is in a valley were there was once a sacred spring.

**The 'Oary Man**: The words of the title and first line occur in an ancient children's game and are a possible corruption of "follow my Gabriel, Holy man" which may refer to a shamanic ritual where a congregation imitated the actions of a dancing priest (Whitlock, *In Search of Lost Gods*, 1979). The circular motion thus evoked seemed appropriate to the minor tradition that links Gabriel to the moon, and all its associations.

**The Leafy Speaker**: The archangel Raphael, the natural healer of disease and of the earth, the patron of writers and revealer of secrets. The counterpart of alchemist/magician deities Thoth and Merlin, his attributes of a broad-brimmed hat and a serpent are also shared by the Roman god of medicine, Mercury.

**The Cloudseeder**: In Jewish tradition, Uriel is the fourth of the archangels who preside over the quarters of the globe. The angel of thunder and earthquakes; in occult lore associated with the planet Uranus, bringer of sudden changes and revolution. The divine messenger who wrestled with Jacob and who warns of the end of the world.

**Lachrimatory**: Cassiel, according to Wenders's *Wings of Desire*, is the angel of "solitudes and tears". The ruling angel of the planet Saturn, he affects karmic matters and the destiny of the human race. The poem is set around Llandaff Cathedral.

**Azrael**: The death-angel, according to the Koran which intermingles Jewish with Gnostic angelologies. In occult tradition, he presides over the planet Pluto, which governs among other things, sex-crime and murder. The counterpart of Anubis, the Egyptian jackal-headed god whose emblem was a blood-stained black and white ox-hide hanging from a pole. I have also identified him with the wolf Fenrir of Norse mythology who swallows the sun and moon at Ragnarøkr and brings on three years of bitter winter.

# Pharmacopœia

*"we cannot emotionally separate a flower*
*from the place or conditions we find it in"*
*(Grigson)*

*for Derrick and Tilla*

**Stinking Iris** *(Iris foetidissima)*
**Kilve**

sea-cliffs &
a green confluence of
waters

daggered leaves
    of flower-de-luce
cut your smile
in slices of salt light

under a fossil
triturate, I conceal
charred letters
for you to dis-
        cover

these stones are shaped by
desire, though you
will not believe it;

it is a country where you are,
a delicate
recurve of tepals

a "pencilling" of purple-gray/
        blue-gray
on tombs at Carnac:

Iris who leads a woman's soul
to the fields of Elysium

"growing more grateful & aromatic
as it dries"

**Cow-wheat** *(Melampyrum pratense)*
**Five Lords' Wood, Quantocks**

visions of finding
the source
among        these juicy
                sluices

*sweat dries*
*& cools as we ascend*

by leaf  by moss   by fern

        fleck

in aqua-
shadow

acts of rapine
on the grass, a
contamination
ground down
to poverty bread

*the strong grip of your hand*
*as you pull me*
*over a dream threshold*

making a *moue*
in the darkness

            (petal-tube)

"hold me
or I will escape you"

**Dog's Mercury** *(Mercurialis perennis)*
**Quaker cemetery, Milverton**

                    bane

of all herbs the most furious

                                        a tendency to
                                        uncultivated land

dark-tongued
the guardians of Acheron

                            in sidereal
                            cadence
                            beyond      possession

snailtrack          birdtrack          spidertrack

                            spark

            a moment's telegnosis

                    root-deep
        in the genesis of silence


**Elder** *(Sambucus nigra)*
**Culbone**

voltage
accrued
since before
Atlantis

leprous crystals
irrupt
each atom, the woods
become hyaline;

incandescent
in shadows of
narcolepsy

Eldrun
or Hyllan-tree

wherein a witch
embarks herself, will

bleed
at midsummer,
reverse
lightning

where
vortices
of 5-petalled flowers
brush lips
skin
hair

by yeast
& muscatel

we are both now

*forspoken*

**Monkey-flower** *(Mimulus guttatus)*
**Lime Street, Stowey**

blood-drop
emlets
in chained water
at our feet

> *(smiley face)*

the "little actor" from
Unalaska
working miles & miles of
> new canals

wild musk
there is none
purer

> the clearest
> of chrome yellow &

most buoyant companion
I could wish for


**Foxglove** *(Digitalis purpurea)*
**Beech hanger, Longstone Hill**

"glistening with excitement"

I eat up your
   delight

in the consummate mathematics of
this many-flowered raceme

*purgeth the body both*
*upwards & down*

invaginated by
"soft felt-like hairs"

        trigger

pin-drop pollenfall &
dazzling cryptographs
    of ultra-violet

        explode

the pyriform
leaving that trace
    of digitoxin

palebuff

        micro-
        crystalline


**Stinging Nettle** *(Urticus dioica)*
**Castle Hill, Stowey**

infesting the
perimeter of the
incendiary field we

lie down in
& fall into the sky

cirrus fibrils a
prolegomenon
to thorms in the S.W.

veins of sorrel & leporine
spoors
& the 2 pale horses
what should *they* signify?

"beset with little prickles"
flagella for the
subjugation of wayward
                        flesh

*(an early photographer of the Linnaean*
*collection having been stung by a nettle*
                        *dried 200 years)*

though makes a good thick
                        soup
heating &
        rich for the blood


**Lady's Bedstraw *(Gallium verum)***
**Quantocks**

decumbent to erect, a complex
                        panicle
& "divers very fine small leaves"

Galen's "cheese-rennet", also termed Gallion
or Pettimugget

seductive flowertrails
penetrate the hills where we confront
the ambiguity of wayposts &
clouds that distil a thin
gleet, where
grass leaps in shoals
before the wind & over the
edge

our words pulled out in strings

"nothing so undefeatable as
large tracts of land"      you say

but this herbe of Venus
it healeth inward wounds

& for washing the feet of persons
tired with overwalking


**Centaury *(Centaurium erythraea)***
**Pontcanna Fields, Cardiff**

tincture of Chiron's blood
among lunar crescents bitten
into turf

Sagittarian moon
peripherals the unconscious

this moment
"resonant as an oboe-reed"
        *with honey*
*to cleanse the eyes from dimness*

at such times
to be with you is enough

                not even to look—

caressing the flower-spikes

yet the immanence of evening
balloons out        convexities
filled with a riverine calm
onto which our windows open

                simultaneously


**Buddleia** *(Buddleia davidii)*
**Elim Terrace, Plymouth**

weather
perfected in

                your kiss

splits
the granite wall
to hexagons of

                quartz

densely plumed

electric secret-
ions in
rain-released
     ozmazone

        the "mantic sill"

tubules cohere
around each droplet

shed
perfume in
lepidopteran
     scales

enters
with ebb & flow of street-talk
the quiet room

          *violaceous*
"the chthonian sphinx presides......."

watching
you fall
in & out of sleep

as easily as peeling

      (on & off)

    a glove

**Tormentil** *(Potentilla erecta)*
**Dartmoor**

            riverpebble

one side sharp
enough to test the
reality of all this          & the body laid to sweat
                           with Venice treacle

              astringent
        the savage crown of tors, sore
        lipped

to macerate in wine
      or wool-fat                branched
                    glabrous or slightly setose
                        gathered in summer, the

             red rootstock

       septfoil                thormantle

"more often creeping"

its vertue to part
all poison from the heart

## Acknowledgements (Contd)

*The Regardians*, printed here in its entirety, was a book published by Odyssey Poets Press (1993). Further thanks are due to Deborah Aguirre Jones for her kind permission to reprint the original images, all of which were created especially for the poems, with the exception of that accompanying 'The Leafy Speaker' which is entitled 'Another Confidante'.

'The Leafy Speaker' featured in the anthology *Earth Ascending: An Anthology of Living Poetry* edited by Jay Ramsay for Stride Publications (1997).

*Portraits of the Artist's Sister*, from which a selection has been made, was published by Odyssey Poets Press (1994). A recording of several of the texts was made at Drive Studios, Swindon on 16th January, 1994, for *Direction Poetry*, Vol. 1.

*Pharmacopœia* was printed as an interim pamphlet by Odyssey Poets Press in conjunction with Terrible Work Press (1999).

Lightning Source UK Ltd.
Milton Keynes UK
UKOW04f1324220913

217655UK00001B/24/P

9 781848 610828